SEVEN *Wonderful* DAYS

The Story of the Creation

BY **FLORENCE JEAN WRIGHT**

Printed in the United States of America

Nashville, Tennessee

ISBN 978-0-9969432-7-7

LOWBAR PUBLISHING COMPANY

Nashville, Tennessee 37204

615-972-2842

E-mail: Lowbarpublishingcompany@gmail.com

For additional information, readings, and seminars,
you may contact the author.

Florence Jean Wright

florencejean40@gmail.com

717-557-1659

Editor: **Michelle**

Content Editor: **Calvin C. Barlow, Jr.**

Graphics & Cover Design By: **Vincent Vi**

Illustration: **Diana_Design**

All rights reserved under the International Copyright Law.
Contents, photos, and cover may not be reproduced in whole or in part in any form
without the expressed written consent of the author or publisher.

Copyright © 2018 by Florence Jean Wright

SEVEN WONDERFUL DAYS
The Story of the Creation

Day 1 (Genesis 1:1-5)
God creates the heavens and the earth.

Day 2 (Genesis 1:6-8)
God creates the sky.

Day 3 (Genesis 1:9-13)
God creates the dry land.

Day 4 (Genesis 1:14-19)
God creates all the stars and heavenly bodies.

Day 5 (Genesis 1:20-23)
God creates all life that lives in the water.

Day 6 (Genesis 1:24-31)
God creates all the creatures that live on the dry land.

Day 7 (Genesis 2:1-3)
God rests.

What an amazing and astonishing world we live in! A world with set routines; with the sun that comes up in the morning, and the moon that comes out at night.

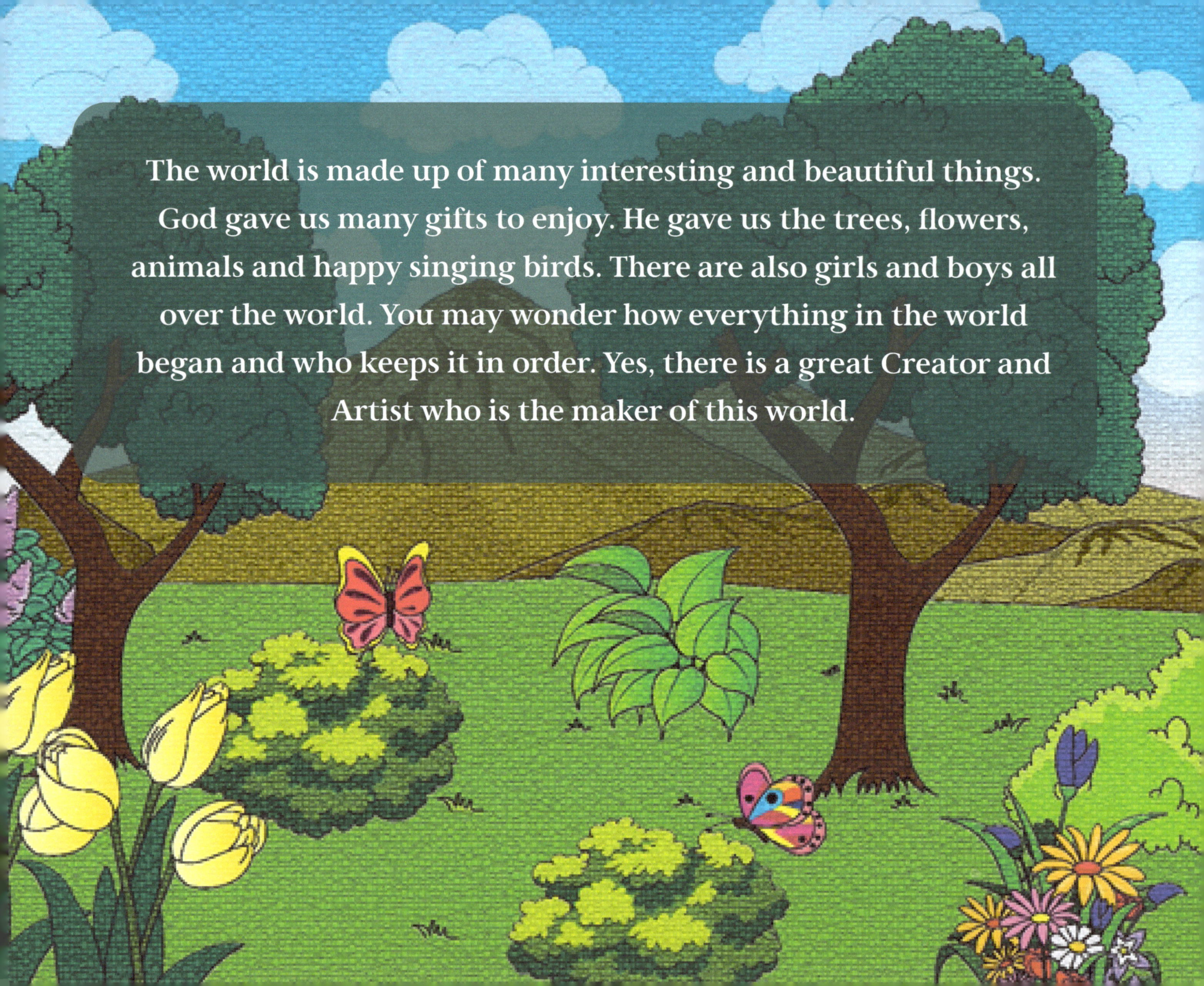

The world is made up of many interesting and beautiful things. God gave us many gifts to enjoy. He gave us the trees, flowers, animals and happy singing birds. There are also girls and boys all over the world. You may wonder how everything in the world began and who keeps it in order. Yes, there is a great Creator and Artist who is the maker of this world.

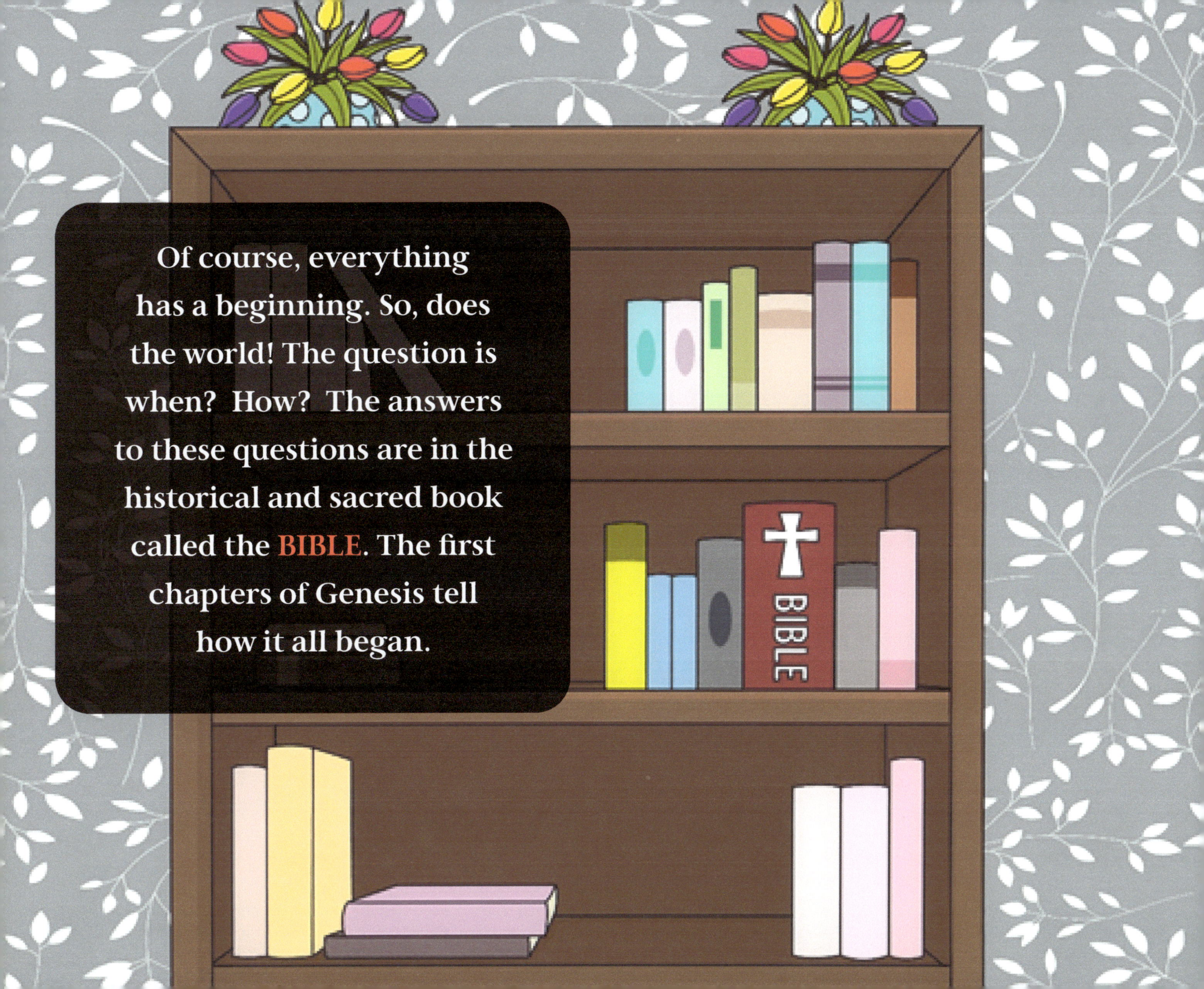

Of course, everything has a beginning. So, does the world! The question is when? How? The answers to these questions are in the historical and sacred book called the BIBLE. The first chapters of Genesis tell how it all began.

The Lord used seven days to create the world as He wanted it to be.
In the beginning, it was very dark.
Water and darkness were the only things in the world
with the Spirit of God hovering over it.

Suddenly, there was a command from God which turned the darkness into light.
This was God's first step toward making the world that we have today into a wonderful and beautiful place.

The FIRST DAY was the beginning of time and history.
Our loving Creator said, *"Let there be light and there was light."*
God called the light Day, and the darkness he called Night.
The first phase of God's creative plan was complete.

Then on the SECOND DAY, silently and miraculously,
the mist on the ocean was drawn up.
Between the mist and the water GOD made what we call the sky,
which is a clear, fresh air forming the "atmosphere,"
or the "firmament" as the Bible calls it.

On the THIRD DAY, GOD spoke again and said, "Let the water under the sky be gathered to one place, and let dry ground appear." GOD called the dry ground "land," and the gathered water He named seas. And GOD said, "That's good!" Then the LORD made a beautiful world and filled it with living creatures, and gave them fresh air to breathe.

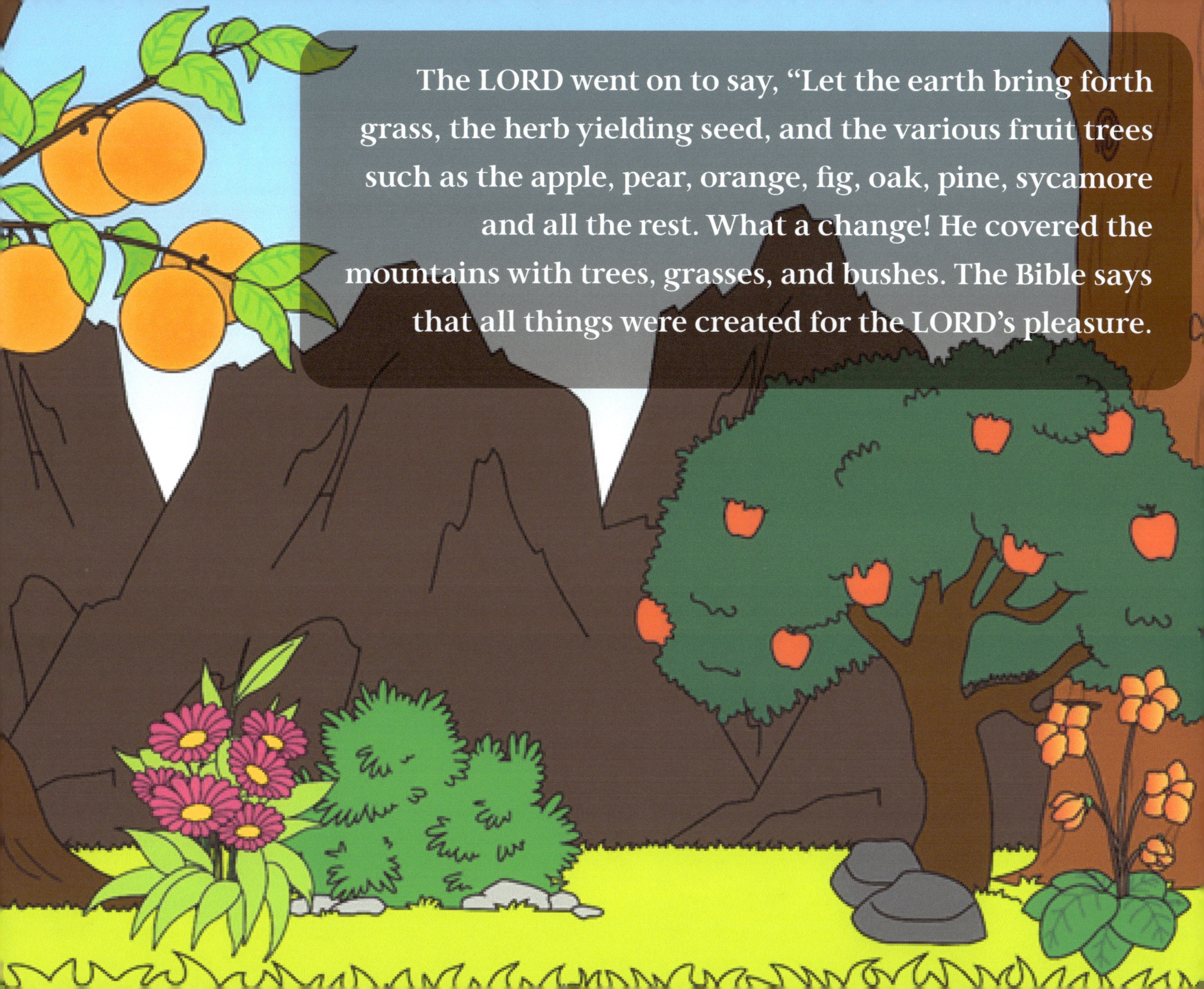

The LORD went on to say, "Let the earth bring forth grass, the herb yielding seed, and the various fruit trees such as the apple, pear, orange, fig, oak, pine, sycamore and all the rest. What a change! He covered the mountains with trees, grasses, and bushes. The Bible says that all things were created for the LORD's pleasure.

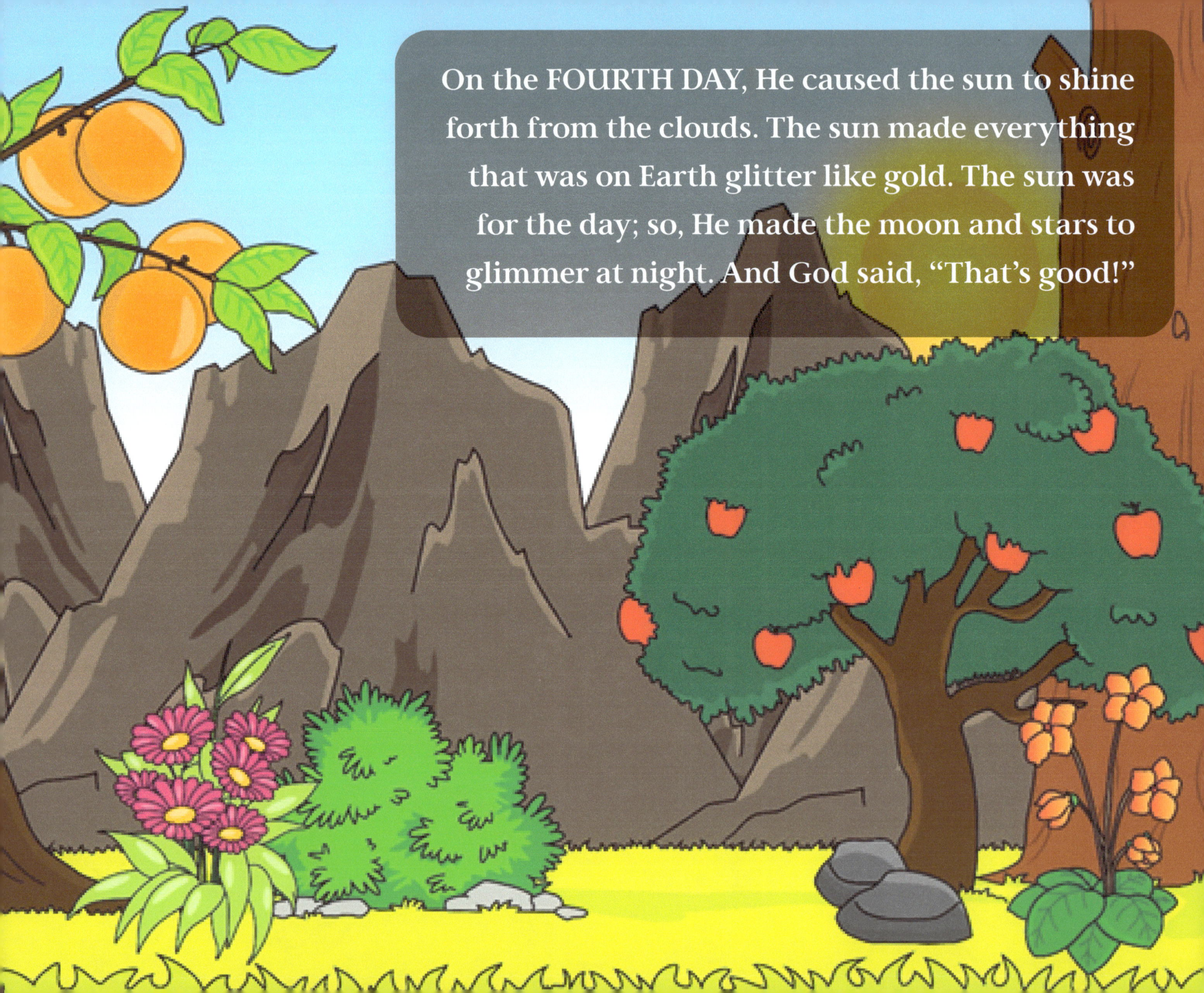

On the FOURTH DAY, He caused the sun to shine forth from the clouds. The sun made everything that was on Earth glitter like gold. The sun was for the day; so, He made the moon and stars to glimmer at night. And God said, "That's good!"

The world was beautiful, but it was also silent and empty of animals and humans. So, on the FIFTH DAY, GOD created fishes and whales for the oceans, lakes, streams, rivers, and seas. He created the birds for the sky. The birds sang for joy, and the silence was broken at last. He also made wild animals. Can you name some of them?

On the SIXTH DAY, GOD made crawling creatures like snakes, lizards, worms, and turtles. GOD made hopping creatures like the grasshoppers, frogs, toads, and kangaroos. Then GOD created an animal with legs like tree trunks, big flapping ears, and on the end of its nose a sort like a long tube. What fun GOD must have had while making the elephant. He also created the horse, zebra, hippopotamus and many more animals as you have seen in the Zoo. He also made pets like dogs and cats, hamsters, and even mice.

Also, on the SIXTH DAY, God created His most fascinating and marvelous present. When everything was ready, GOD said, "Let us make man and woman, in our image, and after our likeness. And let them have dominion over all of the earth".
"And the Lord formed man out of the dust of the ground and breathed into his nostrils and man became a living soul."
God named him Adam.

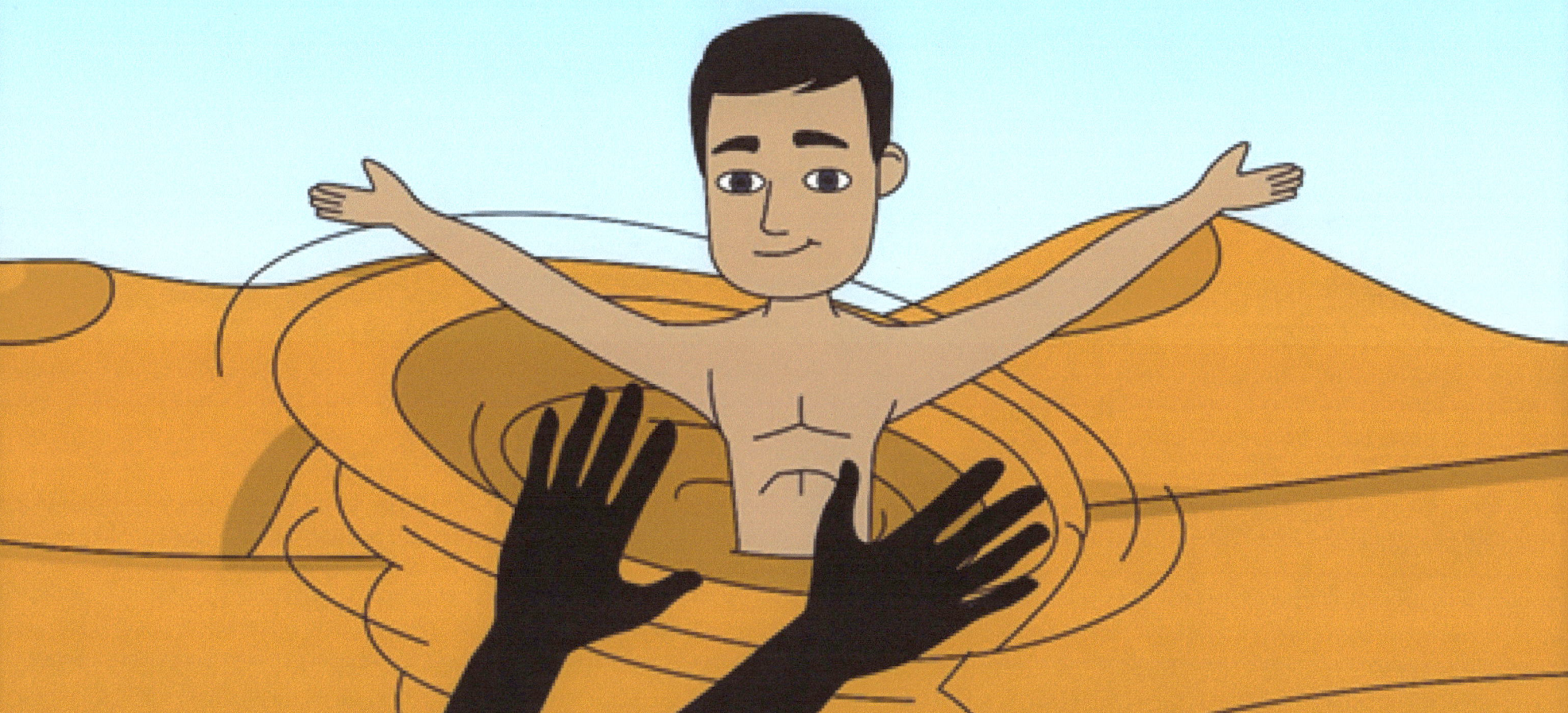

GOD gave Eve to Adam as his wife and gave Adam to Eve as her husband. GOD blessed them and said to them, *"Be fruitful and multiply and take care of the earth and all of its living things."* Later they would have two sons, Cain and Abel. And this was the first family on earth. And, then GOD said, "That's good!"

Then GOD rested on the SEVENTH DAY.

To learn more about this wonderful story, read the book of Genesis in your Bible.

www.ingramcontent.com/pod-product-compliance
Lightning Source LLC
Chambersburg PA
CBHW050855010526

44118CB00004BA/175